To

_____

From

_____

A Christmas Dress for Ellen

RETOLD BY

THOMAS S. MONSON

Illustrated by Ben Sowards

DESERET
BOOK

SALT LAKE CITY, UTAH

Text © 1998 Thomas S. Monson
Illustrations © 2004 Ben Sowards

Art Direction by Richard Erickson. Design by Sheryl Smith.

DESERET BOOK is a registered trademark of Deseret Book Company.

Visit us at DeseretBook.com

Library of Congress Cataloging-in-Publication Data

Monson, Thomas S., 1927-
  A Christmas dress for Ellen / Thomas S. Monson ; illustrated by Ben Sowards.
    p. cm
  ISBN 978-1-59038-386-5 (alk. paper)
  1. Christmas. 2. Service (Theology) 3. Helping behavior—Religious
aspects—Church of Jesus Christ of Latter-day Saints. I. Title.

BV45.M59 2004
242'.335—dc22   2004014566

Printed in the United States of America
Inland Press, Menomonee Falls, WI

10   9   8   7   6   5   4   3   2

Christmas is many things to many people—from the eager, materialistic grasping of a child for a present to the deep spiritual thankfulness of the mature heart for the gift of a Savior. If there is one common denominator, perhaps it is this: Christmas is love. Christmas is the time when the bonds of family love transcend distance and inconvenience. It is a time when love of neighbor rises above petty day-to-day irritations, and doors swing open to give and receive expressions of appreciation and affection.

If to our Christmas gift list is added the gift of service—not only to friends and family, but also to those who badly need help—then our giving can be complete.

Several years ago, Marian Jeppson Walker related to me an experience her family had one Christmas season long years ago. It provides a touching example of the gift of service.

It was December of 1927 in the remote prairie town of Hillspring, Alberta, Canada. A young mother, Mary Jeppson, was getting her five small children ready for bed. Her heart was so full of sorrow and concern that she felt it would surely break. It was Christmas Eve, and all of the children except for the oldest, Ellen, age ten, were dancing around, excited to hang their stockings for Santa to come.

Ellen sat very subdued in a corner of the cold, small, two-room house. She felt that her mother was wrong to let the children build up their hopes for Santa to come, for there would be no Santa. There was nothing to fill the stockings. There would be only a little mush for breakfast. Just a week earlier, the family's only milk cow had died of starvation. The winter had just started, and already it was cold and harsh.

Times were hard, and Ellen, being the oldest, had too much responsibility put on her thin young shoulders. She had become very cynical, and childhood hopes and dreams and excitements had been put out of mind much too early.

Mary helped each one of her children to hang a little darned and mended stocking, but she couldn't persuade Ellen to participate. All Ellen could say was, "Mother, don't do this; don't pretend."

After the stockings had been hung, Mary read to the children the
Christmas story from the Bible and then recited a few Christmas poems
from memory—memories of her own happy childhood.

ow Mary sat alone by the dying fire. Her husband, Leland, had gone to bed several hours earlier, feeling sad and discouraged. Mary knew that he felt he had failed his wife and children. She thought of their plight here in this land of ice and snow. Spring had come very late and winter had come very early for the last two years, causing all of their crops to freeze and fail.

In October Mary had received a letter from her sisters living in Idaho. They told her that they knew times were very hard for her, and although they had suffered some setbacks themselves, they wanted to know what they could send the family for Christmas.

Mary hadn't written back right away. She was reluctant to tell them how poor and destitute the family really was. Finally in November, seeing that things were not going to get any better, in desperation she had written.

ary had requested only necessities. She told them of her family's urgent need for food, especially wheat, yeast, flour, and some cornmeal. She added that it would be a blessing if they could ship just a bit of coal, for it was so cold, and their fuel was down to almost nothing. She asked for some old, used quilts, for all of hers had worn thin and were full of holes, and they could no longer keep her children warm. Also she requested some worn-out pants

to cut up and use to once again patch the pants her boys were wearing. She mentioned their desperate need for socks and shoes and gloves and warm hats and coats. At the close of the letter, she had written, "If you could just find a dress that someone has outgrown, I could make it over to fit Ellen. She is far too somber for such a young girl. She worries so about the family and about our needs. She has only one dress that she wears all the time, and it is patched and faded."

The week before Christmas had found Leland daily hitching up the horse to the sleigh and making the three-hour round trip from Hillspring into the town of Cardston to check at the train station and post office for a package from Idaho. Each day he would receive the same disappointing answer. Finally, on the day of Christmas Eve, he left early in the morning, went into Cardston, and waited for the one daily train. He checked at the post office as well. He left at noon, however, to return home to Hillspring before dark. And he left without a package. As he rode home, he wept openly, knowing how sad Mary would be.

ow, as Mary ceased her reminiscing, she realized how cold she was; the fire in the stove was all but out. The clock on the wall showed that it was 3:30 A.M. She looked up at the sad little mended stockings still hanging empty and felt that her heart was hanging just as empty.

Outside the wind was blowing at about seventy miles an hour, and the snowstorm had intensified. She was about to put out the lantern and go to bed for a few hours when suddenly there was a knock at the door.

Mary opened the door to find a man standing there with his son. For all the world he looked exactly like what she would expect Santa himself to look like. He was covered with frozen snow and ice. For a moment Mary doubted her senses, but then she realized it was George Sidney Schow, the mailman from Cardston. He belonged to the Church, and he knew the plight of the family. He told Mary that he knew of their waiting for the package from Idaho and that he knew there would be no Christmas without it.

George Schow was a good man. A University of Utah graduate, he had years before been stricken with a disease that had caused him to gradually go blind. After receiving a priesthood blessing, he had miraculously regained partial sight in one eye. Although he was unable to work in his chosen profession of engineering, he had found work as a postman to support his wife, Ingeborg, and their eight children.

On this particular day of Christmas Eve, George, with a team of horses pulling his sleigh, had traveled through a violent snowstorm to deliver the mail to half a dozen or more communities near Cardston. When he

returned to the post office that afternoon, he was so cold and exhausted that he ached throughout his body. He longed to settle his horses for the night and join the family celebration in his warm, cozy home. But someone from the train station came by the post office to tell him that ten large crates had arrived from the States for the Jeppson family.

It was about four in the afternoon, but already it was dark. The storm was getting worse. George's horses, shivering with cold, were not capable of making another trip. The mailman decided it was just too late. There wasn't anything he could do about it.

George went home to his eager family. He placed the Christmas tree in the living room, and the children joyfully gathered around to decorate it. Although he was surrounded by happy activity and by the delicious aromas of traditional Danish holiday foods, George could not shake off thoughts of the struggling Jeppson family and the packages waiting at the post office. He took Ingeborg aside, and the couple knelt and prayed for guidance. They decided that the only thing he could do was to take the crates out to the Jeppsons' little isolated farmhouse in Hillspring that very night.

So with a borrowed team of horses and a borrowed sleigh with sharper runners than his own, he set out for the Jeppson place, accompanied by his fifteen-year-old son, Sidney. Ingeborg insisted that Sidney go along; although George's eyesight was passable in the daytime, his wife knew he would not be able to see at night in the midst of a fierce prairie blizzard. Ingeborg and the children sent the father and son on their way with sandwiches and little candies and snacks, and hot rocks were wrapped in blankets to keep their feet warm through the long journey.

George and his son struggled to find their way through the blinding snowstorm. Several times they felt the guidance of the Spirit as they prayed that they would reach their destination safely. With the snowdrifts deepening hour by hour, the horses plodded along more and more slowly. At last they arrived at the farmhouse. They were relieved to see one small light still on in the house.

When George and Sidney entered the home and saw how bare and humble it was, they knew why they had felt so urgently prompted to make the trip. After the postman had told Mary about his decision to come, he and his son brought the crates into the house. Mary insisted that the two stand by the stove to get warm. She got some of Leland's clothes to replace their frozen, wet clothing.

It was nearly five o'clock in the morning when the sleigh headed back into town. It had taken George and Sidney eight hours to get to the Jeppsons' place because of the severity of the storm. They wouldn't get home until noon or later on Christmas day. Mary thanked them both as best she could, but she always said that there just were not words enough to express her thanks. After all, how do you thank a miracle, and a Christmas miracle at that?

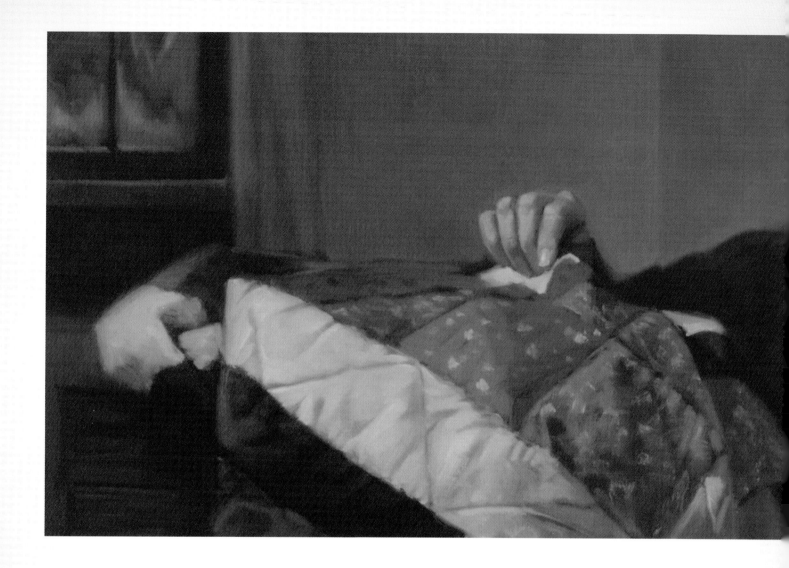

Mary quickly began to unpack the crates, for she had only an hour or so before the children would awaken. At the top of one of the crates she found a letter from her sisters. They told her that quilting bees had been held all over the Malad Valley, and from these, six thick, warm, beautiful quilts had been made for them. They also told of the many women who had sewn shirts for the boys and dresses for the girls, and of others who had knitted warm gloves and hats.

The donation of socks and shoes had come from people for miles around. The Relief Society had held a bazaar to raise the money to buy

the coats, and all of Mary Jeppson's sisters, nieces, cousins, aunts, and uncles in Idaho had gotten together to bake the breads and make the candy to send. There was even a crate half full of beef that had been cured and packed so that it could be shipped, along with two or three slabs of bacon and two hams.

The letter closed with these words: "We hope you have a Merry Christmas, and thank you so much for making our Christmas the best one we've ever had!"

Mary's family awakened that Christmas morning to what to them was a miracle. Bacon was sizzling on the stove, and hot muffins were ready to come out of the oven. There were jars of jams and jellies and canned fruit.

For each boy there was a bag of marbles, and each girl had a little rag doll made just for her. Every stocking that was hanging was stuffed full of homemade taffy, fudge, divinity, and dried fruit of every kind. Later, Mary and Leland were to find tucked in the toe of the stockings that had been sent for them a few dollars with a little note that the money was to be used to buy coal for the rest of the winter.

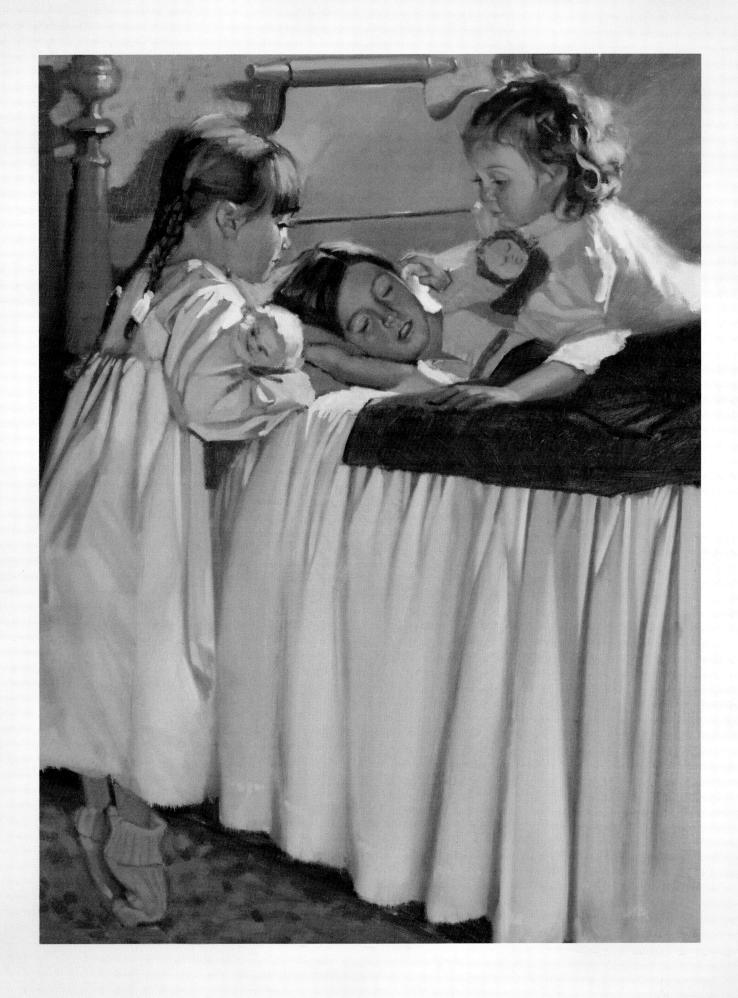

The most wonderful miracle, though, occurred when Ellen, the very last to get up, rubbed her eyes in disbelief as she looked at the spot where her stocking was supposed to have been hung the night before and saw hanging there a beautiful red Christmas dress, trimmed with white and green satin ribbons. She later said it was the most wonderful Christmas ever. That morning, with the Christmas dress for Ellen, a childhood had been brought back, a childhood of hopes and dreams and Santa Claus and the miracle of Christmas.

From a beloved Christmas hymn we recall these lines:

How silently, how silently
The wondrous gift is giv'n!
So God imparts to human hearts
The blessings of his heav'n.
No ear may hear his coming;
But in this world of sin,
Where meek souls will receive him, still
The dear Christ enters in.

May all of us welcome the Savior of the world into our hearts and into our Christmas celebrations. May we experience the joy of setting aside convenience and personal comfort, if need be, in favor of Christian service. Then may we learn, as did an ancient prophet, that when we are in the service of our fellow beings, we are truly in the service of our God.

President Thomas S. Monson told the story "A Christmas Dress for Ellen" at the First Presidency Christmas Devotional in 1997, and an adaptation of his address was published as a Christmas booklet in 1998. The story was related to President Monson by Marian Jeppson Walker (now deceased), a daughter of Mary Jeppson, the mother in the story. Sister Walker and her husband, William, also exchanged correspondence about the story with President Monson over the years. Additional details were obtained through correspondence with descendants of George Schow, the mailman who delivered the long-looked-for packages to the Jeppson family on Christmas Eve. In addition to other family members, those descendants include Mark Schow (now deceased) and Gayla Woolf Holt. The help and information from all these family members is acknowledged and appreciated.